M000078518

A DAILY DOSE OF

MINDFULNESS

*A daily journal for cultivating
mindfulness in your life*

PETER PAUPER PRESS, INC.
WHITE PLAINS, NEW YORK

PETER PAUPER PRESS
Fine Books and Gifts Since 1928

Our Company

In 1928, at the age of twenty-two, Peter Beilenson began printing books on a small press in the basement of his parents' home in Larchmont, New York. Peter—and later, his wife, Edna—sought to create fine books that sold at "prices even a pauper could afford."

Today, still family owned and operated, Peter Pauper Press continues to honor our founders' legacy—and our customers' expectations—of beauty, quality, and value.

Written by Hannah Beilenson
Designed by Heather Zschock
Cover illustration by Sandra Jacobs

Copyright © 2019
Peter Pauper Press, Inc.
202 Mamaroneck Avenue
White Plains, NY 10601 USA
All rights reserved
ISBN 978-1-4413-2947-9
Printed in China
7 6 5 4 3 2

Visit us at www.peterpauper.com

Each moment is just what it is. ...
We could get depressed about it, or we could
finally appreciate it and delight in the preciousness
of every single moment of our life.

Pema Chödrön

*I*t's hard to slow down and be here now. But mindfulness is possible—it just requires us to take a moment each day to be aware of our minds, bodies, and surroundings.

Here are some mindfulness techniques to consider:

• Notice the joys of daily life—the sweetness of a ripe peach, the bassline to your favorite song, the relief after a big sneeze!

• Don't forget to breathe, especially when feeling stressed.

• Accept your emotions as a natural response to life, and appreciate that even "negative" feelings can help you understand yourself better.

• Practice joyful ownership. Hold on only to things you love and need, and let go of what clutters your home and distracts your mind.

• Thank often and thank everything. The trees, the grass, the spider on the wall—the world is nothing without them.

• Practice kindness.

In these weekly pages, take note of mindful moments daily, and in doing so become more present in all your waking hours.

MY MINDFULNESS REFLECTIONS

How I can exercise mindfulness in my life.
What techniques help you practice awareness? What are some ways you can opt out and take time to breathe, notice, feel, and let go?

Ways I can live in the present with others.
Appreciating and communicating with loved ones fosters mindful relationships.

Today's mindful moments: _____ Date: _____

Today's mindful moments: _____ Date: _____

Today's mindful moments: _____ Date: _____

Today's mindful moments: _____ Date: _____

_____

_____

_____

_____

_____

Today's mindful moments: _____ Date: _____

_____

_____

_____

_____

_____

How I practiced mindfulness with others this week: _____

_____

_____

_____

_____

_____

_____

_____

_____

Today's mindful moments: _____ Date: _____

Today's mindful moments: _____ Date: _____

Today's mindful moments: _____ Date: _____

Today's mindful moments: _____ Date: _____

Today's mindful moments: _____ Date: _____

How I practiced mindfulness with others this week: _____

Today's mindful moments: _____ Date: _____

_____

_____

_____

_____

_____

_____

Today's mindful moments: _____ Date: _____

_____

_____

_____

_____

_____

_____

Today's mindful moments: _____ Date: _____

_____

_____

_____

_____

_____

_____

Today's mindful moments: Date:

Today's mindful moments: Date:

How I practiced mindfulness with others this week:

Today's mindful moments: _____ Date: _____

Today's mindful moments: _____ Date: _____

Today's mindful moments: _____ Date: _____

Today's mindful moments: _____ Date: _____

Today's mindful moments: _____ Date: _____

How I practiced mindfulness with others this week:

Today's mindful moments: _____ Date: _____

Today's mindful moments: _____ Date: _____

Today's mindful moments: _____ Date: _____

Today's mindful moments: Date:

Today's mindful moments: Date:

How I practiced mindfulness with others this week:

Today's mindful moments: _____ Date: _____

_____

_____

_____

_____

_____

_____

Today's mindful moments: _____ Date: _____

_____

_____

_____

_____

_____

_____

Today's mindful moments: _____ Date: _____

_____

_____

_____

_____

_____

_____

Today's mindful moments: _____ Date: _____

Today's mindful moments: _____ Date: _____

How I practiced mindfulness with others this week:

This is the real secret of life:
to be completely engaged
with what you are doing
in the here and now, and
instead of calling it "work,"
realize that this is play.

Alan Watts

How I can incorporate less "work" and more "play" in my life:

Today's mindful moments: _____ Date: _____

Today's mindful moments: _____ Date: _____

Today's mindful moments: _____ Date: _____

Today's mindful moments: _____ Date: _____

Today's mindful moments: _____ Date: _____

How I practiced mindfulness with others this week:

Today's mindful moments: _____ Date: _____

_____

_____

_____

_____

_____

Today's mindful moments: _____ Date: _____

_____

_____

_____

_____

_____

Today's mindful moments: _____ Date: _____

_____

_____

_____

_____

_____

Today's mindful moments: _____ Date: _____

Today's mindful moments: _____ Date: _____

How I practiced mindfulness with others this week: _____

Today's mindful moments: _____ Date: _____

Today's mindful moments: _____ Date: _____

Today's mindful moments: _____ Date: _____

Today's mindful moments: Date:

Today's mindful moments: Date:

How I practiced mindfulness with others this week:

Today's mindful moments: _____ Date: _____

Today's mindful moments: _____ Date: _____

Today's mindful moments: _____ Date: _____

Today's mindful moments: _____ Date: _____

Today's mindful moments: _____ Date: _____

How I practiced mindfulness with others this week: _____

Today's mindful moments: _____ Date: _____

Today's mindful moments: _____ Date: _____

Today's mindful moments: _____ Date: _____

Today's mindful moments: _____ Date: _____

Today's mindful moments: _____ Date: _____

How I practiced mindfulness with others this week: _____

Today's mindful moments: _____ Date: _____

Today's mindful moments: _____ Date: _____

Today's mindful moments: _____ Date: _____

Today's mindful moments: _____ Date: _____

Today's mindful moments: _____ Date: _____

How I practiced mindfulness with others this week: _____

By simply accepting
your life exactly the way
it is...you are letting
go of all resistance.
You are freeing yourself
from your negative emotions.

Sonia Ricotti

Ways I can free myself of negative emotions:

Today's mindful moments: _____ Date: _____

_____
_____
_____
_____
_____
_____

Today's mindful moments: _____ Date: _____

_____
_____
_____
_____
_____
_____

Today's mindful moments: _____ Date: _____

_____
_____
_____
_____
_____
_____

Today's mindful moments: _____ Date: _____

Today's mindful moments: _____ Date: _____

How I practiced mindfulness with others this week: _____

Today's mindful moments: _____ Date: _____

Today's mindful moments: _____ Date: _____

Today's mindful moments: _____ Date: _____

Today's mindful moments: _____ Date: _____

Today's mindful moments: _____ Date: _____

How I practiced mindfulness with others this week:

Today's mindful moments: _____ Date: _____

Today's mindful moments: _____ Date: _____

Today's mindful moments: _____ Date: _____

Today's mindful moments: _____ Date: _____

Today's mindful moments: _____ Date: _____

How I practiced mindfulness with others this week: _____

Today's mindful moments: _____ Date: _____

Today's mindful moments: _____ Date: _____

Today's mindful moments: _____ Date: _____

Today's mindful moments: _____ Date: _____

_____

_____

_____

_____

_____

_____

Today's mindful moments: _____ Date: _____

_____

_____

_____

_____

_____

How I practiced mindfulness with others this week: _____

_____

_____

_____

_____

_____

_____

_____

Today's mindful moments: _____ Date: _____

_____
_____
_____
_____
_____
_____

Today's mindful moments: _____ Date: _____

_____
_____
_____
_____
_____
_____

Today's mindful moments: _____ Date: _____

_____
_____
_____
_____
_____
_____

Today's mindful moments: _____ Date: _____

Today's mindful moments: _____ Date: _____

How I practiced mindfulness with others this week: _____

Today's mindful moments: _____ Date: _____

Today's mindful moments: _____ Date: _____

Today's mindful moments: _____ Date: _____

Today's mindful moments: _____ Date: _____

_____
_____
_____
_____
_____
_____

Today's mindful moments: _____ Date: _____

_____
_____
_____
_____
_____

How I practiced mindfulness with others this week: _____

_____
_____
_____
_____
_____
_____

When the sun rises
the whole world dances
with joy and everybody's
heart is filled with bliss.

D. T. Suzuki

My idea of a blissful day:

Today's mindful moments: _____ Date: _____

Today's mindful moments: _____ Date: _____

Today's mindful moments: _____ Date: _____

Today's mindful moments: Date:

Today's mindful moments: Date:

How I practiced mindfulness with others this week:

Today's mindful moments: _____ Date: _____

Today's mindful moments: _____ Date: _____

Today's mindful moments: _____ Date: _____

Today's mindful moments: Date:

Today's mindful moments: Date:

How I practiced mindfulness with others this week:

Today's mindful moments: _____ Date: _____

Today's mindful moments: _____ Date: _____

Today's mindful moments: _____ Date: _____

Today's mindful moments: Date:

_____

_____

_____

_____

_____

_____

Today's mindful moments: Date:

_____

_____

_____

_____

_____

_____

How I practiced mindfulness with others this week:

_____

_____

_____

_____

_____

_____

Today's mindful moments: _____ Date: _____

Today's mindful moments: _____ Date: _____

Today's mindful moments: _____ Date: _____

Today's mindful moments: _____ Date: _____

_____

_____

_____

_____

_____

_____

Today's mindful moments: _____ Date: _____

_____

_____

_____

_____

_____

How I practiced mindfulness with others this week: _____

_____

_____

_____

_____

_____

_____

Today's mindful moments: _____ Date: _____

Today's mindful moments: _____ Date: _____

Today's mindful moments: _____ Date: _____

Today's mindful moments: _____ Date: _____

Today's mindful moments: _____ Date: _____

How I practiced mindfulness with others this week: _____

Today's mindful moments: _____ Date: _____

_____

_____

_____

_____

_____

_____

Today's mindful moments: _____ Date: _____

_____

_____

_____

_____

_____

_____

Today's mindful moments: _____ Date: _____

_____

_____

_____

_____

_____

_____

Today's mindful moments: _____ Date: _____

How I practiced mindfulness with others this week: _____

*By taking good care of
the present moment, we
take good care of
the future.*

Thich Nhat Hanh

How I can be more present:

Today's mindful moments: _____ Date: _____

Today's mindful moments: _____ Date: _____

Today's mindful moments: _____ Date: _____

Today's mindful moments: _____ Date: _____

Today's mindful moments: _____ Date: _____

How I practiced mindfulness with others this week: _____

Today's mindful moments: _____ Date: _____

_____

_____

_____

_____

_____

_____

_____

Today's mindful moments: _____ Date: _____

_____

_____

_____

_____

_____

_____

_____

Today's mindful moments: _____ Date: _____

_____

_____

_____

_____

_____

_____

Today's mindful moments: _____ Date: _____

_____

_____

_____

_____

_____

_____

Today's mindful moments: _____ Date: _____

_____

_____

_____

_____

_____

How I practiced mindfulness with others this week: _____

_____

_____

_____

_____

_____

_____

Today's mindful moments: _____ Date: _____

_____

_____

_____

_____

_____

_____

Today's mindful moments: _____ Date: _____

_____

_____

_____

_____

_____

_____

Today's mindful moments: _____ Date: _____

_____

_____

_____

_____

_____

_____

Today's mindful moments: Date:

Today's mindful moments: Date:

How I practiced mindfulness with others this week:

Today's mindful moments: _____ Date: _____

_____

_____

_____

_____

_____

_____

Today's mindful moments: _____ Date: _____

_____

_____

_____

_____

_____

_____

Today's mindful moments: _____ Date: _____

_____

_____

_____

_____

_____

Today's mindful moments: _____ Date: _____

_____

_____

_____

_____

_____

_____

Today's mindful moments: _____ Date: _____

_____

_____

_____

_____

_____

_____

How I practiced mindfulness with others this week: _____

_____

_____

_____

_____

_____

_____

_____

Today's mindful moments: _____ Date: _____

_____

_____

_____

_____

_____

_____

Today's mindful moments: _____ Date: _____

_____

_____

_____

_____

_____

_____

Today's mindful moments: _____ Date: _____

_____

_____

_____

_____

_____

_____

Today's mindful moments: _____ Date: _____

Today's mindful moments: _____ Date: _____

How I practiced mindfulness with others this week: _____

Today's mindful moments: _____ Date: _____

Today's mindful moments: _____ Date: _____

Today's mindful moments: _____ Date: _____

Today's mindful moments: _____ Date: _____

_____

_____

_____

_____

_____

_____

Today's mindful moments: _____ Date: _____

_____

_____

_____

_____

_____

How I practiced mindfulness with others this week: _____

*I am a lover of what is,
not because I'm a spiritual
person, but because it hurts
when I argue with reality.*

Byron Katie

Ways to accept what I cannot change:

Today's mindful moments: _____ Date: _____

_____

_____

_____

_____

_____

_____

Today's mindful moments: _____ Date: _____

_____

_____

_____

_____

_____

_____

Today's mindful moments: _____ Date: _____

_____

_____

_____

_____

_____

_____

Today's mindful moments: _____ Date: _____

_____

_____

_____

_____

_____

_____

Today's mindful moments: _____ Date: _____

_____

_____

_____

_____

_____

_____

How I practiced mindfulness with others this week: _____

_____

_____

_____

_____

_____

_____

Today's mindful moments: _____ Date: _____

Today's mindful moments: _____ Date: _____

Today's mindful moments: _____ Date: _____

Today's mindful moments: _____ Date: _____

Today's mindful moments: _____ Date: _____

How I practiced mindfulness with others this week: _____

Today's mindful moments: _____ Date: _____

Today's mindful moments: _____ Date: _____

Today's mindful moments: _____ Date: _____

Today's mindful moments: _____ Date: _____

Today's mindful moments: _____ Date: _____

How I practiced mindfulness with others this week: _____

Today's mindful moments: _____ Date: _____

Today's mindful moments: _____ Date: _____

Today's mindful moments: _____ Date: _____

Today's mindful moments: _____ Date: _____

_____

_____

_____

_____

_____

_____

Today's mindful moments: _____ Date: _____

_____

_____

_____

_____

_____

_____

How I practiced mindfulness with others this week: _____

_____

_____

_____

_____

_____

_____

Today's mindful moments: _____ Date: _____

Today's mindful moments: _____ Date: _____

Today's mindful moments: _____ Date: _____

Today's mindful moments: _____ Date: _____

Today's mindful moments: _____ Date: _____

How I practiced mindfulness with others this week:

Today's mindful moments: _____ Date: _____

_____

_____

_____

_____

_____

_____

Today's mindful moments: _____ Date: _____

_____

_____

_____

_____

_____

Today's mindful moments: _____ Date: _____

_____

_____

_____

_____

_____

_____

Today's mindful moments: _____ Date: _____

Today's mindful moments: _____ Date: _____

How I practiced mindfulness with others this week: _____

Be mindful.
Be grateful.
Be positive.
Be true.
Be kind.

Roy T. Bennett

How I can improve my outlook on life:

Today's mindful moments: _____ Date: _____

Today's mindful moments: _____ Date: _____

Today's mindful moments: _____ Date: _____

Today's mindful moments: Date:

Today's mindful moments: Date:

How I practiced mindfulness with others this week:

Today's mindful moments: _____ Date: _____

Today's mindful moments: _____ Date: _____

Today's mindful moments: _____ Date: _____

Today's mindful moments: Date:

Today's mindful moments: Date:

How I practiced mindfulness with others this week:

Today's mindful moments: _____ Date: _____

_____
_____
_____
_____
_____
_____

Today's mindful moments: _____ Date: _____

_____
_____
_____
_____
_____
_____

Today's mindful moments: _____ Date: _____

_____
_____
_____
_____
_____
_____

Today's mindful moments: _____ Date: _____

_____

_____

_____

_____

_____

_____

_____

Today's mindful moments: _____ Date: _____

_____

_____

_____

_____

_____

_____

_____

How I practiced mindfulness with others this week: _____

_____

_____

_____

_____

_____

_____

_____

Today's mindful moments: _____ Date: _____

_____

_____

_____

_____

_____

Today's mindful moments: _____ Date: _____

_____

_____

_____

_____

_____

Today's mindful moments: _____ Date: _____

_____

_____

_____

_____

_____

Today's mindful moments: _____ Date: _____

Today's mindful moments: _____ Date: _____

How I practiced mindfulness with others this week: _____

Today's mindful moments: _____ Date: _____

Today's mindful moments: _____ Date: _____

Today's mindful moments: _____ Date: _____

Today's mindful moments: _____ Date: _____

_____
_____
_____
_____
_____
_____

Today's mindful moments: _____ Date: _____

_____
_____
_____
_____
_____
_____

How I practiced mindfulness with others this week: _____

_____
_____
_____
_____
_____
_____

Today's mindful moments: _____ Date: _____

Today's mindful moments: _____ Date: _____

Today's mindful moments: _____ Date: _____

Today's mindful moments: _____ Date: _____

Today's mindful moments: _____ Date: _____

How I practiced mindfulness with others this week:

Looking at beauty in the world is the first step of purifying the mind.

Amit Ray

Observations on the beauty around me:

Today's mindful moments: _____ Date: _____

Today's mindful moments: _____ Date: _____

Today's mindful moments: _____ Date: _____

Today's mindful moments: _____ Date: _____

Today's mindful moments: _____ Date: _____

How I practiced mindfulness with others this week: _____

Today's mindful moments: _____ Date: _____

_____

_____

_____

_____

_____

_____

Today's mindful moments: _____ Date: _____

_____

_____

_____

_____

_____

_____

Today's mindful moments: _____ Date: _____

_____

_____

_____

_____

_____

_____

Today's mindful moments: _____ Date: _____

_____

_____

_____

_____

_____

Today's mindful moments: _____ Date: _____

_____

_____

_____

_____

_____

How I practiced mindfulness with others this week: _____

Today's mindful moments: Date:

_____

_____

_____

_____

_____

_____

Today's mindful moments: Date:

_____

_____

_____

_____

_____

_____

Today's mindful moments: Date:

_____

_____

_____

_____

_____

_____

Today's mindful moments: Date:

_____

_____

_____

_____

_____

Today's mindful moments: Date:

_____

_____

_____

_____

_____

How I practiced mindfulness with others this week:

Today's mindful moments: _____ Date: _____

_____

_____

_____

_____

_____

_____

Today's mindful moments: _____ Date: _____

_____

_____

_____

_____

_____

_____

Today's mindful moments: _____ Date: _____

_____

_____

_____

_____

_____

_____

Today's mindful moments: Date:

_____

_____

_____

_____

_____

Today's mindful moments: Date:

_____

_____

_____

_____

_____

How I practiced mindfulness with others this week:

_____

_____

_____

_____

_____

Today's mindful moments: _____ Date: _____

_____

_____

_____

_____

_____

Today's mindful moments: _____ Date: _____

_____

_____

_____

_____

_____

Today's mindful moments: _____ Date: _____

_____

_____

_____

_____

_____

Today's mindful moments: _____ Date: _____

_____
_____
_____
_____
_____
_____

Today's mindful moments: _____ Date: _____

_____
_____
_____
_____
_____

How I practiced mindfulness with others this week: _____

_____
_____
_____
_____
_____

Today's mindful moments: _____ Date: _____

_____

_____

_____

_____

_____

_____

Today's mindful moments: _____ Date: _____

_____

_____

_____

_____

_____

_____

Today's mindful moments: _____ Date: _____

_____

_____

_____

_____

_____

_____

Today's mindful moments: _____ Date: _____

Today's mindful moments: _____ Date: _____

How I practiced mindfulness with others this week: _____

The happiness of
your life depends
upon the quality of
your thoughts.

Marcus Aurelius

Ways to clear and focus my mind:

Today's mindful moments: _____ Date: _____

Today's mindful moments: _____ Date: _____

Today's mindful moments: _____ Date: _____

Today's mindful moments: _____ Date: _____

Today's mindful moments: _____ Date: _____

How I practiced mindfulness with others this week: _____

Today's mindful moments: _____ Date: _____

Today's mindful moments: _____ Date: _____

Today's mindful moments: _____ Date: _____

Today's mindful moments: _____ Date: _____

_____

_____

_____

_____

_____

_____

Today's mindful moments: _____ Date: _____

_____

_____

_____

_____

_____

_____

How I practiced mindfulness with others this week: _____

_____

_____

_____

_____

_____

Today's mindful moments: _____ Date: _____

Today's mindful moments: _____ Date: _____

Today's mindful moments: _____ Date: _____

Today's mindful moments: _____ Date: _____

_____

_____

_____

_____

_____

Today's mindful moments: _____ Date: _____

_____

_____

_____

_____

How I practiced mindfulness with others this week: _____

_____

_____

_____

_____

_____

Today's mindful moments: _____ Date: _____

Today's mindful moments: _____ Date: _____

Today's mindful moments: _____ Date: _____

Today's mindful moments: _____ Date: _____

_____

_____

_____

_____

_____

Today's mindful moments: _____ Date: _____

_____

_____

_____

_____

_____

How I practiced mindfulness with others this week: _____

_____

_____

_____

_____

_____

Today's mindful moments: _____ Date: _____

Today's mindful moments: _____ Date: _____

Today's mindful moments: _____ Date: _____

Today's mindful moments: _____ Date: _____

Today's mindful moments: _____ Date: _____

How I practiced mindfulness with others this week: _____

Today's mindful moments: _____ Date: _____

_____

_____

_____

_____

_____

Today's mindful moments: _____ Date: _____

_____

_____

_____

_____

_____

Today's mindful moments: _____ Date: _____

_____

_____

_____

_____

_____

_____

Today's mindful moments: _____ Date: _____

_____

_____

_____

_____

_____

Today's mindful moments: _____ Date: _____

_____

_____

_____

_____

_____

How I practiced mindfulness with others this week: _____

The thinking mind is
what is busy. You have to
stay in your heart....
The rest is up here in
your head where you are
doing, doing, doing.

Ram Dass

Ways I can slow down and enjoy the present:

Today's mindful moments: _____ Date: _____

_____

_____

_____

_____

_____

_____

Today's mindful moments: _____ Date: _____

_____

_____

_____

_____

_____

_____

Today's mindful moments: _____ Date: _____

_____

_____

_____

_____

_____

_____

Today's mindful moments: Date:

Today's mindful moments: Date:

How I practiced mindfulness with others this week:

Today's mindful moments: _____ Date: _____

_____

_____

_____

_____

_____

_____

Today's mindful moments: _____ Date: _____

_____

_____

_____

_____

_____

_____

Today's mindful moments: _____ Date: _____

_____

_____

_____

_____

_____

_____

Today's mindful moments: _____ Date: _____

Today's mindful moments: _____ Date: _____

How I practiced mindfulness with others this week: _____

Today's mindful moments: _____ Date: _____

Today's mindful moments: _____ Date: _____

Today's mindful moments: _____ Date: _____

Today's mindful moments: _____ Date: _____

_____

_____

_____

_____

_____

Today's mindful moments: _____ Date: _____

_____

_____

_____

_____

_____

How I practiced mindfulness with others this week: _____

Today's mindful moments: Date:

_____

_____

_____

_____

_____

_____

Today's mindful moments: Date:

_____

_____

_____

_____

_____

_____

Today's mindful moments: Date:

_____

_____

_____

_____

_____

_____

Today's mindful moments: _____ Date: _____

Today's mindful moments: _____ Date: _____

How I practiced mindfulness with others this week: _____

Today's mindful moments: _____ Date: _____

Today's mindful moments: _____ Date: _____

Today's mindful moments: _____ Date: _____

Today's mindful moments: _____ Date: _____

How I practiced mindfulness with others this week:

Today's mindful moments: _____ Date: _____

Today's mindful moments: _____ Date: _____

Today's mindful moments: _____ Date: _____

Today's mindful moments: _____ Date: _____

How I practiced mindfulness with others this week: _____

When you wash your hands, when you make a cup of coffee, when you're waiting for the elevator— instead of indulging in thinking, these are all opportunities for being there as a still, alert presence.

Eckhart Tolle